MW00454432

Happy Retirement!

SUPURE CREATIVES

How did we do?

Good! Yeah... Please take some time to review us. It really helps our business and also other customers in making a decision. Thanks!

Not good! We're so sorry. Contact us: SupureCreatives@gmail.com & give us a chance to fix it...

To submit a review:
1. Go to the product detail page for the item on Amazon.com.
2. Click **Write a customer review** in the Customer Reviews section.
3. Click **Submit.**

SUPURE CREATIVES

amazon.com/author/HappyRetirement

If you have any question - contact us: **SupureCreatives@gmail.com**

Made in United States
North Haven, CT
19 May 2022

19338310R00062